YOU A
ENOUGH
JUST BE YOU!

Why? Because
I Believe in YOU!

By Suzie Welstead

Author: Suzie Welstead Title: YOU ARE ENOUGH JUST BE YOU!—Why? Because I Believe in YOU!

As a child I was given a different name and went by the nick name Suki. I legally changed my name to Suzie when I became an adult. For simplicity I will be using Suzie throughout this book.

Dedication

I dedicate this book to Patrick Welstead for his unfaltering love and support, and for giving me the freedom I have always desired.

Acknowledgments

First and foremost, thank you to me for stepping up
and stepping out to write this book.

I would like to acknowledge the 3 men in my life
who are the foundation of my world.

I would also like to acknowledge the...

People who helped me along the way including
friends and family, you know who you are.

Samaritans for their immediate support.

Places for victims of domestic violence
and the one that sheltered me for 6 months.

I'd like to offer a personal thank you to everyone who made
this book possible especially Linda Vettrus-Nichols
and her husband Terry (Earthwind) Nichols,
my online mum and dad.

A huge thank you to my kickass online sister,
Michelle Catanach author of
*Uncaged: The Rise of the Badass— 26 Stories of the
Wild Woman to Ignite the Fire in Your Soul,*
for starting me on story writing and making my chapter in her book
available for the introduction here in my book.

Table of Contents

INTRODUCTION: PRAYING FOR TIME

Chapter 1: Love Yourself for the Person You Are 15

Chapter 2: Trust in Yourself 18

Chapter 3: Love on Yourself 20

Chapter 4: Believe in Yourself 22

Chapter 5: Be Unstoppable 29

Chapter 6: Get Out of Your Own Way 33

Chapter 7: Fly Like a Bird 36

Chapter 8: Be Free in Your Mind 39

Chapter 9: Never Give Up 43

Chapter 10: You Can Only Control You 46

Chapter 11: Move On 49

Chapter 12: Keep Yourself Fully Present 52

About the Author

INTRODUCTION: PRAYING FOR TIME

Hanging on to hope
When there is no hope to speak of
And the wounded skies above say it's much, much too late
Well, maybe we should all be praying for time

~ *George Michael*

It was 25th December 2016 11.20pm. I'd had a beautiful Christmas day with my two boys and husband. Christmas had always been difficult as my birth family were no longer a part of my life. But I was so grateful to have my own family; they were more than enough.

I was heading downstairs when my eldest son stopped me in my tracks. 'I have some news you're not going to like'. As I turned towards him with a blank stare he said, 'George Michael is dead'.

An 'oh my gosh' tumbled out of my mouth and a very loud, 'Noooo'!

I stumbled down the stairs. Dear God, let this be a mistake. But it was true. My idol, my legend, my hero, my saviour during tough times was gone.

LIVING ON THE STREETS
As I mentioned earlier, Christmas was a difficult time for me. Home life was unbearable. I was isolated, controlled; I needed to break free. I desperately craved the freedom to

do what I wanted, say what I wanted, and be who I desperately wanted to be. I had tried - and failed –to leave many times. I knew I couldn't take the physical, mental and emotional abuse anymore.

I had arrived home from school and started making the tea, like always. Then I started preparing the meal. Cooking dinner for the family always fell on me. Tonight, I was my making my favorite meal - chips, beans and runny fried eggs. Then the urge hit me. The bliss got the best of me and I decided to leave home. This time for real. AND just like that, I made up my mind. There was no going back.

I finished cooking the last meal in that house. Grabbing my white school satchel, I added a roll of toilet paper, my diary, a pen and 20p. Then I shouted up the stairs that I was leaving and ran out of the house. Where was I going? What was I going to do to survive? I didn't know. I just knew I had to run and run I did.

It must have been about 11.30 pm when I started panicking. I had never been on my own in the streets at night. I could hear people coming out of the pub, and I froze. Oh gosh, what do I do? I was terrified. I ran to the phone box and, after scuffling through my bag for the 20 pence, I rang a friend or two to see if they could help me. They said no. They knew I was in a bad place and that helping me would bring shame on them and their families. I was all alone.

Luckily I had the telephone number for the Samaritans in my diary. I must have had the foresight to jot the number down when I saw it at school. I rang the number, in a state of panic and overwhelm, mixed with relief and freedom. I had escaped, yet I was fearful of where I would end up or what might happen to me. The Samaritans reassured me that everything would be okay. They kept me talking until a taxi collected me and took me to a refuge. A shelter for women and children who had suffered domestic abuse.

LOST AND ALONE

It felt strange to be in a new room, somewhere unfamiliar...
yet safe. I couldn't believe I'd done it, that I'd left. I hadn't
planned it, but I guess I was at my tipping point.

At 17, I was solely responsible for cooking, cleaning and all
other household chores on top of going out to work with
the added blow that I wasn't allowed to keep my wages. I
knew I'd made the right decision but my mind was in
overdrive - thinking, panicking, excited, scared - I'm
amazed I got to sleep.

I awoke to a loud banging on the main door of the shelter.
It startled me; my heart jumped into my throat. I grabbed
my duvet and listened at the door to my room. I was
relieved when I realised it was just a husband looking for
his wife. I sat back on the bed and, whether through shock
or just the realization of what I had been through, I cried. I
cried my little heart out. Tears fell and kept rolling down
my face. And then I realised why I was crying so hard: No
one had come for me!

That knock on the door made me believe that someone was
coming for me, that they were looking for me, that they
wanted me back. I felt that maybe, just maybe, someone
cared. But they didn't. And the truth was that they never
did. Was I that bad? Was I so unlovable that no one
wanted me? I had never felt so worthless, unwanted, and
alone.

CLINGING TO HOPE

The following morning, I woke up feeling hopeful with a
deep knowing that I could do this. I knew there was no
going back! A support worker came to my aid with a
toothbrush and toothpaste. I will never forget how
supportive and understanding she was. She asked if I
wanted to ring home and made it clear that I didn't have to

go back there and could stay at the refuge for 6-months. It was one of the hardest phone calls I've ever made in my life. I was nervous, sweating profusely, and so glad that this was not happening face-to-face.

My mum answered. I recall saying her name and thinking how little affection there was between us. She told me to come home, telling me it would all be forgotten. I told her I wasn't coming back. And that was it. She said she never wanted to see me again and that I was dead to her, and then slammed the phone down... affirming to me that I'd done the right thing.

The next six months passed by like a whirlwind. I felt I was living someone else's life. All I'd ever known was my mum's control and expectations, so I didn't know who I was meant to be or what I was supposed to do. Every time I went out, I felt I had to look over my shoulder for fear of bumping into someone that knew my family or me.

I wanted to understand why I wasn't loved, why I wasn't wanted. I turned to my family doctor. Evidently me being a girl meant I was rejected the moment I was born. I already had an older sister. Boys were highly revered in my family's culture. I was told that my parents had hoped for a son. My brother was born a few years later. This confirmed why I always felt like the odd one out in the family – unloved, unwanted, and anything but special. My mother never hugged me or told me that she loved me.

A few days later I bumped into a family friend. She seemed shocked to see me. I wanted to know if my family had mentioned me, still desperately clinging to hope that maybe they did miss me and loved me after all. Only it wasn't to be. This woman let me know that my mum had told her and everyone else, that I had died in a car crash. My world once again came 'crashing' down. I started to question everything. I locked myself away until my 18th birthday when I was finally ready to face the world.

PRAYING FOR TIME

On 8th September 1988, I turned 18 in a houseful of strangers who made me feel so special. I felt like, all my birthdays and Christmases had come at once! I was never given a birthday card or present living at home yet these beautiful people, in spite of hardship, had saved up and created a birthday that I would never forget. They had bought me a small stereo system for playing tapes and records, as well as cards, food, vodka, and anything they could think of to make my day special.

I was immensely grateful even though I struggled to express this outwardly. I had no idea how to react, as no one had ever done anything like this for me before. Here I was, in a room full of strangers who were singing happy birthday to me, like they'd known me my whole life, and something my family had failed to do. I was touched and felt honoured to have them all in my life. *Praying For Time*, by George Michael started to play and I knew that in time, everything would be okay.

You see, George was there again like he always had been, comforting me with his words and music. When his songs played, it was as if he was with me, the power of his lyrics and tunes were always easing my pain.

Now that I was 18 and an adult, I had to start making important decisions about my life. It was time to move on from the refuge, leave the city and start a fresh. There was another woman about to leave the refuge as well. She mentioned that she was looking for a lodger. She lived on the outskirts of the city and was happy for me to move in with her as long as I found a job and paid my way. So that is what I did.

I contacted my brother to bring me some clothes from home, he was the only link I had to my old life. After he delivered my clothes, I left the city with my new landlady. I found a job in my new town and babysat for my landlady when she went out. I paid my way and did the best I could. As I made new friends, I started to look for somewhere else to live. I wanted to feel safe and secure because at one point, I felt I had outstayed my welcome.

For a while I flitted here and there, moving from place to place as I tried to find some where I could establish some roots to call home. No matter where I went, I never entirely belonged. I lost most of my music collection and my stereo from all the moving around. At times I felt I knew what I wanted while at other times my life felt as if I was standing still waiting for someone to give me direction.

FINDING LOVE
Finally, I found a friend who I felt I could trust... who introduced me to her mum who was so caring and kind, it touched my heart. Even though they took on lodgers, they didn't have room for me at the time. I felt so lost and desperately unhappy where I was staying, so they invited me to visit on many occasions. One day they invited me over, and while I was there one of the lodgers announced that she was moving out. Without hesitation, my friend asked if I wanted to move in. I replied with a hug and ecstatic YES!

I moved in and for the first time I felt that I belonged, that I finally had somewhere that I could call home. I was made to feel welcomed and cared for, and that meant more than words can ever describe.

We had lots of fun together, lots of laughter. We looked out for each other, went partying together; life was incredible. My 21st birthday was a pivotal moment in my life. I felt happy, free, and full of hope. Despite my past, I had a future that I could look forward to. And who would have thought that only six-months later I would meet the man who would become my husband and father of my children, and that we'd create the family life that I'd desperately craved as a child.

Chapter 1
LOVE YOURSELF FOR THE PERSON YOU ARE

My name is Suzie. I'm a certified happiness life coach for trauma survivors and victims of domestic violence. I love to guide, empower, and inspire my clients to achieve their full potential. I hold a safe space for them so they can discover themselves. I believe in people. There are many people who unfortunately do not believe in themselves. When somebody believes in you, you can actually believe in yourself too. It always makes a difference when you start believing in yourself because you start becoming the real you. The real, passionate, loving, amazing person that you are. And you are amazing. Everybody's amazing!

I never used to trust myself because I never used to believe in myself. The more you start working on yourself, the more you start knowing that it's okay to be you; you become the amazing person you were meant to be on this planet.

That's how I feel about life. And I love what I do. I love building people up. I love to inspire them. I like to motivate them. I offer my knowledge and personal experience in order to motivate and inspire them. I like to encourage people to become their best.

I had been in denial for so many years. I used to try and sugar coat my life with the idea that everything is hunky dory and sunny. It was on the outside, however on the inside, I was battling with myself. I was forever fighting with myself because the distinctions I was making were not true for me.

For instance, after making myself homeless at the age of 17, knowing that I had to go and couldn't tolerate living there anymore, I started punishing myself. Even though I was fed up with the emotional, mental, and physical abuse that I had suffered, I started believing that what I did was wrong. When it wasn't wrong! I wanted connection, I wanted a perfect family, and it wasn't a perfect family.

I wanted love and a relationship. A really good relationship! And I was never, ever going to get it from home. That's what I wanted. That's what I felt and desired. And I guess that's the starting point of when I left home to start making a life, my life.

We all have choices. You either turn left or right. The choice is yours. Even if you turn left and it wasn't supposed to be left, you're still going to get where you intended to go. It just takes a bit longer.

I've had this urgency to do stuff, because that's what society teaches us, that you must do this, do this, do this, and you're listening to all the outside world, following other people.

I was 17 and homeless. I didn't know where I was going to go with this. I wanted my family, but knew they didn't want me, and so I just kept chugging along, making this life for myself. I started helping people. I ended up working for the National Health Service in England (NHS), in mental health. It started to make me realize that I probably have down moments but I didn't want to admit to them. I also worked with disadvantaged teens, helping them to love themselves and develop life skills.

I moved on to helping young people and children, survivors and victims of domestic violence. Domestic abuse is very close to my heart because that's obviously something I suffered from, and I know what it's like when you can't trust the ones around you.

We believe that they are the ones who are our role models; then we realize that they are not. The damage is so deep. It's just so wrong. As kids, we believe they are the ones for us. That they know better than we do. We think we don't know anything and suffer the consequences in our adult lives.

It took me years to process the truth. Once you start to trust yourself, you are no longer dependent on others.

Chapter 2
TRUST IN YOURSELF

I used to let people walk all over me. I used to do, do, do, and say, yes, yes, yes to everybody! My boundaries were shit. And I mean shit...

There were times when I'd overeat, instead of sitting with myself. I didn't want to sit with me. I didn't want to be with me. I didn't want to do anything that I liked because I didn't feel like I deserved it or was worthy. Once you start trusting and it does take time, you can fly!

You can fly to the sky and back. You are the sky, you know. There are no limits. There are no limits when you start trusting yourself. You just follow what you want to do and it's great.

Keeping myself a prisoner of my past produced many heartaches. Even though I met an amazing man, who has been my husband for the past 25 years, I tried to sabotage that relationship; yet he stood tall. He always stood by me.

We have two amazing, beautiful boys. I can't say boys anymore because they are now young men. But they are my boys. And it's beautiful. It's great! All along, this is what I wanted; I was given what I wanted! The sabotage came from crucifying myself with the thoughts like, "I should have done this or that" and "Oh my gosh, what if my mum finds out." and "Oh my, what can I do?"

I didn't have to DO anything. I didn't HAVE to do ANYTHING! Because my actions were stronger than what I was thinking. I've created this beautiful family. A beautiful home. And this business that motivates and inspires people to just be themselves.

You are enough. You're amazing! It's time to unfold and unwrap all the garbage that you put onto yourself, because it's not worth it anymore.

You get to strive forward. You get to start creating what you want, which can be very, very difficult if you have always done what others wanted you to do. However, there are ways. There are great ways! I have included some of them in this book. When you know them, you'll follow them. Once you start, everything becomes easier. You will relax into yourself and have the ability to calm yourself. You can now become anything and anyone.

Chapter 3
LOVE ON YOURSELF

I know it sounds cliché, we say it all the time. Love yourself! Otherwise, nobody will, so love yourself. Nobody will love you if you don't love yourself. I never used to get that. I used to think 'of course I love myself', but I didn't! Loving yourself is so crucial.

The first step to loving myself was to be honest with myself. For years and years, although I am very open and honest, I wasn't open and honest with me or my story.

I never had a hug or a kiss from my mum as a child. When you come from a background of trauma and a family like I had, you may start thinking, "Well, actually, I don't need hugs and kisses and love." That was true for me.

In reality, you do. Because, you're a kid. How are you going to grow and expand unless you get the most important ingredients to your life, which is love?

Love is like water, it fills our empty places.

~Deanne Michelle Welsch

Love can be shown through actions. Love can be heard through words. But when you've never heard those loving words, when you've never had those loving actions, you start believing you don't deserve it.

And as soon as you get a bit of a flavor for it, Woah! You think, this is not my zone. You put all your barriers up and you think, nope, this isn't for me. I'll kill it off somehow. And you start finding ways to sabotage your relationships or your friendships, or your work life, because you think, "I don't deserve it, anyway."

If your own mum cannot say, "I love you," who else will? It's not until you get older that you start to realize that you don't need anybody's approval or permission, because that's what you're waiting for, your mum to approve and give you that permission.

Something must have driven me since I was very young. Because what has gotten me here? What has gotten me here is some kind of inner strength within me, a part of me that I did love. Yet I was covering it up with all this stuff that I believed I was supposed to be doing, when all I had to do was love on myself. Truly tell myself 'I love you'.

When you come from a background like I had, you've always got this little patter on your shoulder that's constantly giving you crap? Giving you the negative words? The words that you don't want to use or even think about. When you hear them enough, you start believing them, because they start coming to you at a very young age. Self-worth is so, so important, and so many of us lack self-worth. Self-worth is developed by every individual person from a very young age. By seven, that is when your self-worth is crucial to build upon.

Chapter 4
BELIEVE IN YOURSELF

If your self-worth had not been built upon while you were growing up, you become vulnerable and can easily step into victim mode because, you were a victim. Your self-talk turns to, "I don't deserve this. I'm not worth it." I'm very lucky to have my husband who was willing to show me what real love is like. I didn't even believe in it before I met him. Well, I guess I thought the world was after me and always questioned, who would love me? My family didn't love me, so who am I expecting to love me? That's how my thoughts operated most of my life. Like a victim. Well yeah, I was a victim.

At this point, I do believe that my trauma was bad enough, that I blocked everything out. I can't even remember my brother or my sister being in the house. I remember that I did speak to my sister about leaving home, and she said, "No, no, you can't do that. As far as my mum goes, we don't know if she's narcissistic or something. As a society we hear so much about it and the victims of those behaviours. They think they love themselves, but they are insecure like a 3-year-old and don't really know how to love themselves. They are not going to teach their kids to love that's for sure.

We definitely lived in a house without love. My siblings had freedom. I felt like a prisoner. I was isolated, I was controlled, I was cooking and cleaning. I felt like a slave. I can say that, today.

I wasn't allowed to have friends. I wasn't allowed to go out. I wasn't even allowed to buy what I wanted to wear or be who I wanted to be. That's why it's so important that this book gets out into the world, because I believe I'm not the only person on this planet who has experienced abuse and its outcomes.

My mum never did drugs or alcohol. I think she was a prisoner to her own thoughts. I think so. But again, that's assuming. My parents divorced when I was 2 years old. She had told me she needed to divorce him because he was an alcoholic and violent. It was an arranged marriage. She had 3 toddlers by the time she was 21 years old. He died when I was 18. I found out from a Social Worker 9 years later.

When I was 27 years old, my sister contacted me to let me know she'd be coming to England to visit my mum and my brother. My brother was still living at home at the time. I agreed to see her and I picked her up down the street from my mum's house. She stayed for an overnight visit with my husband and I. We only had Shane at the time, I was pregnant with Alex. Our boys were born about 22 months apart. I dropped her off in front of the house and headed back home. My sister flew back to Canada and a few days later I received a call from my brother asking if he could see his nephew. I said, "Yes, of course." I put the phone down and said to my husband, Paddy, I'll go as long as you are by my side. He agreed and I made arrangements with my brother to stop by the house, knowing full well I'd also be seeing my mother.

My mum greeted me at the door with a hug, she gave Paddy a hug too. She made tea for us and served it in her best china. It was awkward. As we were leaving my mom handed me 50 pounds and I said, "I'm not here for the money." She pushed it at me and said, "It's for my grandson." At that moment I knew to not say anything, put it in my purse and just accept it. So, I did. The visit was over and we agreed to meet up again.

I got excited thinking we might actually be a family. It was October and Christmas was just around the corner. A month later I called her, keeping my promise that we would see her again. I asked her what she wanted Shane to call her, grandma, nan, nanny. She said, "Leave us alone, you're happy, you've got your family." I said, "Pardon?' and she said, "Leave us alone, I have nothing for you, I have no money, no nothing." I said, "I don't want anything, you're my mum, and I just want us to be a family." "What about your grandchildren?" I said. She replied with, "There are plenty of children out there without grandparents." Then she hung up and I was left devastated. I felt like I was banging my head against a brick wall, and for what? She threw away her own grandchildren!

Twenty years later my sister got in touch with me and my brother and told us that she wasn't getting any younger and that we needed to connect. We connected on Facebook. My brother and I started texting. That's how I found out that my brother never knew my mum had cut me off. He thought I didn't care about them.

A few months later we decided to start meeting up in the city. On one of those occasions he said, "I bet you wouldn't want to meet up with mum?" and I said, "Sure I would, why not?" He still lived with my mum. That's when I found out he didn't know what had happened all those year ago. We arranged a date and time for me to stop by the house. My mum seemed surprised I was there, she called out my name and then she cried. She said, "I'm sorry, he hit me, I hit you." I assumed she meant my dad. I showed her photos of my boys. While we were sitting on the couch, she noticed that my was hair was short. It was short when I saw her at age 27, perhaps she hadn't noticed or didn't remember and she said, "Oh, I wish I could cut my hair and drink." So, I assume that's what she thinks that's what I did when I left home. Because my hair was right down to my bum when I left. I had spoken of alcohol during our visit when I was 27. I'd go and have a pint, from that visit she knew that I drank when I socialized, and that's what she said.

I thought, "Oh, is that what you think then? Life will be great if you cut your hair and have a beer? But I didn't question it. I didn't want to. It wasn't for me to question. Although I did think to myself, if only you knew mum how damaged and insecure I have felt most of my life because of you.

There were a lot of times when she went into a frenzy. I think she just went on a mad attack. And as a kid, you're thinking to yourself, "I just want her to be happy. If she has to beat the shit out of me, let her beat the shit out of me, because I just want her to be happy." So, you let it happen the once, thinking, "Right, it'll be okay now. She'll be all right, now. She's done what she needs to do."

The problem is, I became numb to it because it was on a regular basis. It wasn't just a one off.

I was her punch bag. I don't think she actually felt she could do enough harm with her hands, that's why she always used instruments or found a broom, a stick or found something that she could attack me with. This was probably the way she was able to detach from the fact that she was actually the one hurting me, not the stick or the broom. And it was quite brutal, at times. She drew blood. But again, I assume it was how she was thinking. After years of covering for her, I wanted to talk about it. From my experience, I believe it's very important to talk about it with someone you trust. The problem is, who can you trust? I have felt stuck and stagnated in my life because of my past, as I didn't know how to express how I really felt or whom I could trust.

People notice if there are bruises. When I went to school, they were well hidden.

We know how swearing at a child is part of emotional abuse. The scars and bruises they are not as apparent. What the swearing does is to create the emotional stuff. When you feel that you're crap and you can't do anything, you withdraw into yourself. You believe that you are not good enough.

There were a couple of incidents I remember quite clearly. Number one was when we lived in a maisonette, a house with two apartments one above the other. I'm not sure what I was doing or how old I was, but I could hear her. When you are living on egg-shells, you tend to tip toe around so your perpetrator doesn't go into a frenzy. And when you've done nothing or you don't know what you've done, you literally shit yourself. In my case, I got hot and felt sick. I just knew what was coming and had no control over it. This was anxiety speaking, this was real. I had no idea how to stop the physical abuse apart from numbing myself.

Yeah, that's what you do, you're in panic mode. Right? Because you can't figure out what's going to happen. You're so numb to it because it happens on a regular basis. You don't even react, you just stand there.

This was one of those incidents where I could hear her coming down from upstairs and I thought, "Oh my God, what have I done. What have I done!" I was in the kitchen and all I could hear was, "You've had a biscuit out of the tin." I thought, "Well, no, I've not."

And she kept saying, "Tell me the truth, tell me the truth, because you're going to get it!" And I'm like thinking, "Oh my gosh, no, I've not had a biscuit! I've not had a biscuit!" And you're really trying to justify that you've not had a biscuit, there's no crumbs, there's no... you know?

And whack, whack, whack, whack, whack. There was an umbrella handy. And she was whacking away on me with it. She pierced my skin. There's still a scar on my wrist. I was thinking, 'oh my God' she drew blood, is she ever going to stop?

You feel so defeated because you're telling the truth. I wasn't even the type of kid who would take a biscuit from the jar and I certainly wasn't a liar. If that's what it's like living inside your house, how the hell are you going to trust living out in the real world? And so, you stay.

As I mentioned earlier, my mum used to have these frenzied attacks on me. She used to literally, bang my forehead against a brick wall. And I mean a brick wall. She used to get so, so angry. I had said she never used her hands, but she did. She would literally grab the back of my head and bang, bang, bang the front and even the sides of it on the wall. I have scars on the sides of my head to this day,

I don't know what the reasons were that would get her so fired up. One day when my head started bleeding, she took her scarf off and burnt it, creating hot ashes that she used to stop the bleeding. She put it onto my forehead to cover up the blood. The bleeding stopped, and it just left a red mark.

In the Indian, Sikh, community, you wear a two-piece suit. So, you've got trousers and you've got a top. And then you've got this really flimsy, thin scarf that they wear around their necks and they cover their heads with it. That's what she used, that's what she burned. I guess it was a way that she didn't have to take me to the hospital or anything. That way she didn't have to admit to what she had done. Same as the other incidents, I knew that it was coming.

After that incident I started thinking about leaving. There was no way I could stay in that house, anymore. This was not love. This was not what I wanted.

Chapter 5
BE UNSTOPPABLE

For me being unstoppable means to never ever give up.
Even on the shitty days. Just get up and do something.
Because those are the days that you need to just do it.
You've got to keep believing in yourself and move on.
You're the one who can be unstoppable. Don't wait for
somebody else to come and tell you this. Do your own
thing, your own way.

One day when I came home from school, my mother told
me to change out of my school clothes and into my ethnic
clothing, my Punjabi suit. I was quite anxious, I was pretty
sure she had set something up. My suspicions were
confirmed when she told me we were going to see Auntie,
our local match maker.

My dad was from Kenya, Africa and my mum was from
Punjab, India and grew up in the Sikh community. After a
ceremony of marrying my father via a picture of him, she
was put on a plane to meet him in England. He was flying
in from Kenya to meet her. They settled into a Sikh
community in England. She raised us within that same
community.

I knew it, she had set up a proposal invitation with the
Auntie. As I entered the Auntie's home, I was given a tray
of tea and told to go into the lounge and serve it to the 30
something year old man who was there waiting for me.

I did and after serving the tea I sat down across from him, stared off into the distance and picked at my nose. I didn't want him to think I was interested in him.

As a 15-year-old, you're wondering, what the hell is he looking at, while he looks you up and down and then stares at you.

He's looking you over in order to decide if you've got any potential to be his wife.

When we got back into the car, my mum started a sing-song, "You're, going to get married, you're going to get married."

Two weeks later the Auntie let my mum know that the man was not interested in me. I was very happy and relieved to know that my mum had no idea I had done my best to turn him off.

I used to work in a factory on the weekends and after school, with my mum. Our boss would always give her my wages. I never used to see my wages! Even when I was 17, I got no money.

I wanted to buy my sister something for her wedding. We were never very close, because we weren't taught to be close or build a healthy relationship. We were quite distant. But I wanted to buy her a little something to let her know that this was from her sister and every time she'd look at it, that's what she'd remember.

I was treated like Cinderella, I couldn't attend my sister's wedding, for whatever reason. My mum just said, "You've got ugly feet," or something, so I wasn't allowed to go to my sister's wedding purely because I had ugly feet? Hmmmm.

But I haven't got ugly feet. They were big. Does that make them ugly? Like I said, we didn't know what was happening in her mind.

At 17, I confronted her one day about her not giving me my wages. Oh my gosh, it was the wrong thing to say. Whoosh. Bang. Lots of slapping and kicking. Then she got a loafer shoe, which is a flat shoe, and she whacked me straight in my eye and my eye bulged out. I got a massive black eye out of the deal.

Another beating. So, what do you do? You just go and clean yourself up. Get to bed, because there's nothing else for you to do. The following morning, she wanted me to run errands, and I said to her, "What, like this?" That was the first time that I thought, she actually felt guilty.

"I'll go," she says. When she got back, she gave me magazines and sweets. Bloody hell I thought, was it Christmas? My family had never celebrated Christmas or my birthday, but I got all of this stuff that day from my mum. She did the errands that she had wanted me to do.

A few hours later, we had a visitor, our social worker who had stopped by for a regular visit. When she saw my black-eye she said to me, "Oh my gosh! What happened to you?" I was just about to tell her and my mum said, "The boys were playing golf outside and the ball hit her in the eye." I felt so defeated.

I must have really mirrored my mum or I must have really looked like her, or I must have really, really resembled something about her that she needed to try and destroy, which was me.

So, I think we were very, very much alike. I got up every time. I just got up. I didn't give up. I just got up. There is a

Japanese Proverb that says, "Fall 7 times, stand up 8". I was delighted when my book in 30 Days coach Linda Vettrus-Nichols told me about it.

Fall 7 times, stand up 8

-Japanese Proverb

I have always loved the number 8. It is similar to the infinity symbol. Fall and get up, fall and get up. If a baby can do it, so can you! If I can do it, so can you! Right?

I'm still giving this woman the time of day because she's my mum. It takes years, doesn't it? Especially when you've been in denial. On my part there is a great deal of closure as I continue to understand myself and my life from a healthy place of detachment.

I guess that's what I am finding out now working with Linda. We originally spoke three years ago when I was still sugar coating a lot of my story. Then I wrote it out in a chapter for Michelle Catanach's book, *Uncaged: The Rise of the Badass*. I realized that I couldn't be telling people that I could help them when I couldn't even help myself and I have this burning passion to help people.

So, I got some therapy and then decided to write this book, which has been quite therapeutic for me. I feel free after going through this process. It wasn't easy writing this book even though Linda's system is quick and efficient. There were days when my head hurt or I didn't feel safe putting so much out there for everyone to see. I went through a huge transition indeed!

Chapter 6
GET OUT OF YOUR OWN WAY

We all need to invest in ourselves in order to grow into the people that we need to be and to stop getting in our own way. There are times when we look around at others and ask questions like, "Well why doesn't he react like that? or "Why didn't that happen for me as well?"

It can all happen. If only you'd get out of your head and start focusing on what you want. When you start believing that you deserve good things, you start being grateful and positive. We've all got these traits. Yet, we don't use them.

The outside world teaches us that if we have this, this, and this, then everything's great.

No. No. No!

Focus on you. Focus on you and stop comparing yourself to everyone else. Get what you want. Make sure your words are clean. Make sure everything sits well with you. If you've been through shit, let yourself know. Write it out. Speak it out.

I couldn't stop myself. I had to say things. I had to let my truth out. Do what you need to do to put it away. Flow it out of your system and start moving forward.

You know, there's a strength that we all have, and that's what keeps us going. There's a hidden strength that probably even I might feel as if I'm Wonder Woman, you know? I've got this real good superpower. That's the only thing that's gotten me through from the beginning. Being the kid witnessing violence and being violated myself, to where I am today.

I am a huge believer in not changing anybody or fixing anyone and I mean that. YOU don't need fixing or changing. YOU just need to be able to understand what you went through and what you are going through now.

To have met a man who doesn't treat me any way out of the ordinary. Never controls. I have so much freedom. It's unbelievable. To be able to say what I want and do what I want. Initially, I caused chaos in our relationship because of my past insecurities. I've been so, so lucky. The more I trust myself the more our relationship grows stronger. YOU see it was never about him, his upbringing was totally different from mine.

I get stronger and stronger, the more I understand and love myself for who I am. For the words that I speak, they have meaning, they have purpose, because I love me. I love who I am and what I do. I say it now and I believe it now. Finally.

In the past I had issues with my husband, so many times. I used to think, "Stick up for me!" But it wasn't about him. It was about me. I had to realize that about me. Because we can all try and blame somebody else. If we come out of trauma or when we're in those situations, we can't think, "Me, me, me" all the time.

You'll always find a solution if you're looking for it. But if you don't seek one, you'll end up deeper and deeper in the chaos, thinking there's no way out. Plus, you end up refusing to look for or at that way out, even if you find it. You just believe at the end of the day that's, that, I'm trapped.

It takes time to become unstoppable. When that time comes, you will fly like a bird.

You won't need anybody to fix you. I've always told my clients, "I'm not here to fix you. I'm not here to change you. Nobody needs fixing. Nobody needs changing. Nobody needs controlling."

You just need to understand yourself better. The best way possible. And the people you meet are the people who will help you do just that, which means getting yourself to understand you. And that's all you need to do.

You've been through trauma, yes, let's talk about it. Let's understand it, how have you seen it? How have you felt it? How did it made you feel? When you start to answer these questions, you can become the best version of yourself.

Chapter 7
FLY LIKE A BIRD

You can fly like a bird. Barriers will start melting away. I have always had such a huge heart, but it was surrounded by ice. Every time I got knocked back. Ice. Every time I had a memory. Ice. Every time I felt like moving forward, my Ego was there to keep me safe. It's the part of me that was too afraid to fly.

As soon as you start making friends with your Ego, and saying, "You know what? It's okay. We've got this. We can do this." Your Ego will settle down.

FEAR
You get to speak to yourself about fear. For starters, ask yourself if it is really fear. What are you feeling? The thing is, we don't like to question ourselves. We'll just go and eat or we'll go and have a pint or something. Instead, ask yourself these questions, "Am I really scared? If the answer is YES, then ask, "What am I scared of?"

Another great question is, "How can you fear something that does not exist?" Change that channel. You're creating fear by your thoughts.

You're creating a horror story in your mind that does not exist. Change the channel. Create a love story. Create a comedy.

Are you in fear? No? What are you creating? A love story of your life? I step out one step at a time. One second at a time. And I trust that everything is good. I believe that instead of feeling the fear that stops us, it's all about courage.

Take that courage, love you and love your life.

Mindfulness has been fantastic for me. When you create a mindfulness practice, you know, I am a fan of Eckhart Tolle. When I first used to listen to him, I had to switch him off because his voice was so slow and I used to think, "Oh my gosh, I've come from this fast, fast, fast, do, do, do! I can't listen to him for five more seconds! He takes like five minutes to say a few words!"

But in reality, you have to stop. You have to stop and think to yourself: I really need to stop doing and just be. That's the only time when you really, really feel that true essence of who you are and who you are meant to be. You are not meant to do, do, do as we see in social media. Do this, do that. Wait. No. Stop. Stop a minute. Stop and stand back, reflect. Notice how you feel. Notice where you are in your life and decide where you'd rather be.

Noticing is massive. It's all about taking note. Notice what you're allowing in your life. When somebody says something to you and it pisses you off, don't just blow it off and say, "That's okay."

No, no, no. Start thinking to yourself: Why is this annoying me? Have a word with yourself. When your words become self-sabotaging, stop. Set a timer. Whatever you need to say, take ten minutes and let 'it rip', just let it go.

LET GO
Do you know why it's okay not to be okay? Only you know what you've been through. So, if you're going through a tough time, let yourself know that it is okay as long as you don't stay there forever.

We don't do that naturally and instead turn ourselves inwards for days, and days, and days. When I didn't want to talk to people, my thoughts were crucifying to me.

I was suffocating with my own thinking. And I didn't know how to stop.

These things take time. They are healthy habits. These habits will become amazing for you once you start using them. When your trust is way off, you find that you really can't trust yourself. Find people you trust, people who believe in you. The ones who as soon as they meet you, they perceive the beauty that is within you.

Only then will you start taking step-by-step actions. Don't be afraid to invest in yourself. It's not about confidence, it's about finding who you are and making that creative change.

You don't have to pretend. Just be happy with yourself.

Chapter 8
BE FREE IN YOUR MIND

Once you start a mindfulness practice, there comes a day when you say to yourself, "Oh my gosh! That person's not pissing me off anymore. What the hell is happening!"

Well, you have obviously taught yourself how to let go. Eckhart Tolle says, for instance, 'if something has really been pissing you off and you can't seem to let go of it, just sit with it.' I start writing it down. That person's really, really pissed me off! I'm angry! I'm agitated! Okay, just accept it. No, I can't accept it, that person is driving me bloody mad!

Then say and/or write, I'm accepting that I'm angry. I'm agitated about this person/situation and I'm letting go. I believe that you are drawn to what will help you the most. Besides Eckhart Tolle, I was drawn to the Ho'oponopono, which is a Hawaiian forgiveness ritual.

In my mind and after journaling my true feelings, I tell the person I'm writing about, "I love you, please forgive me, I'm sorry, thank you." And that's a good way to keep the peace, by consistently using that as a mantra. So, even if things do show-up you're working on them subconsciously.

The Ho'oponopono cleaning process consists of repetitions of the following phrases:

I Love You

Please forgive me

I am sorry

Thank you

Your mind is never going to forget anything. Start using the tools that you've picked up along the way to help you become a better person. It's all about trusting yourself to move forward. Trusting that even when shit happens, it's meant to be. There is a lesson to be learned so receive it.

That's why I say reflecting on things is really good. Start observing what you do. Don't get attached to everything, detach yourself. Stand back and reflect on what is happening, then see what you can do to shift things.

Sometimes we're like a bull in a China shop. We'll get in there, we'll start arguing and whatever, but if we actually stand back and watch, rather than take action in the moment, it's ever so powerful.

Never be afraid to go home and write in your journal about what happened or write down how you feel about things.

You know, everybody has their own way of dealing with stuff. Start becoming your own observant hero. Stop being a victim, wake up a hero, instead. Know that everything that you do is good, even when it's not good. Ask yourself what you have learned from it? It's all about learning and remembering, you know? It's easy to think 'oh, I've won, I've lost, I've won, I've lost.'

No, no, no. Always think of everything as a win-win. Edison invented the light bulb. He made lots of mistakes. He didn't consider them mistakes, just valuable learning experiences. I say, either I win or I learn. What you need to do then is get yourself a really pretty journal, something that you want to write in. Use your favorite pens and pencils and start drafting how you're feeling and how you've become your own problem solver.

I've felt stuck so many times that I've been able to help people unwrap their minds.

Unwrap your mind. Unfold it. And start creating with the good stuff in there. Self-care is very important. It's the little things we do for ourselves that can make the biggest difference in life.

Spend some time on your own for one hour a day, doing what you want to do. Put away your phone. Turn off the TV or watch a comedy for an hour if that is what you really want to do.

If you want to go out and walk. Walk.

If you want to ring your friend. Do it.

Do something for yourself that means something to you.

Go on YouTube and watch interesting videos.

Put your headphones on and listen to some calming music.

Sit there holding a crystal if it's crystals.

Sit there with a picture of a special friend or memory.

Look at your vision board and just dream away.

Think about all the beautiful traits of the people you love. The positive virtues that we all have, like kindness, compassion, love, and peace. Ponder on them before you go to bed. Do you know what I mean?

Chapter 9
NEVER GIVE UP

Never, ever give up. Please, please, please never give up. Even if you get right down to that crunch where you just feel that you really can't do it anymore, be honest with yourself and say, "I really can't do this right now." At that time, you can't see it, but within minutes or days, you might get a flash of inspiration from somebody who comes to see you or while talking with someone on the phone. You might get something from somewhere that just makes you open your eyes and think, "Oh gosh, I matter, I can do this." Also notice what is going on around you when you are in a funk. You could be led to a place that is going to help you, not hinder you. Try it!

I've been there, when I didn't want to be there. But actually, it was a cry for help. I didn't know how to support myself. I didn't know how to love myself. I just wanted to be seen and heard.

It's never about likes. It's never about status. It's about the difference you make in the world.

Wake up and be your own bloody hero. Only you know what you can be.

Wake up and listen to the birds sing.

The quickest way to focus on the here and now is to use all your senses.

When you notice yourself drifting, think, what am I looking at with my eyes, what can I smell, what am I feeling, who am I speaking to?

SET YOUR INTENTIONS

- Decide what YOU want for YOU

- Make the shift a reality

- Become empowered

- Take responsibility

- Change your story from what is holding you back to where you want to be

MAKE PEACE WITH WHO YOU ARE

- Focus on what matters to you, your feelings and emotions

- Learn to forgive yourself for past mistakes

SELF-CARE, SELF-LOVE

- Be Your Own Superhero

- It is Just Around the Corner

- Take the Next Step

- Believe to Achieve

- Give to Yourself

- Be Who You Are

- Release the Baggage

- Keep it Simple

- Find Simple Solutions & Easy Techniques

- Be More Mindful

- Learn to accept what is and to give permission to yourself to make this a reality

Chapter 10
YOU CAN ONLY CONTROL YOU

Everything was against me. I had an incident at school and the school still sent me home. I said I didn't want to go home, I'm going to get beat up. Nobody was listening.

We had social services. They weren't listening. And then, when I was 17, they said to me, "You know, Suzie, if you just tell us what's going off?" And I thought, hold on a minute! You've been witnessing this for 17 years and now you're telling me to admit it to you?

You're telling me 'we can do something now, if you say something Suzie'? You've been watching my fucked-up life for 17 years and now you want me to tell you something? I didn't say those words, but I sure was thinking them.

Before you finally trust yourself, you are in a victim mode. You don't believe that anyone is going to help you, because the ones who were 'supposed' to love and care for you, didn't love and care for you so how is anybody else going to do it?

I was a social drinker as I got older and the kids were my main responsibility,

I used to get flashbacks and memories. I didn't want to drag up all this rubble from the past so I numbed it out and used drink as my companion...until I got to a stage where I just had enough of drinking, it wasn't fun anymore. I was using it as a coping mechanism.

BANISH THE FEAR

- FEAR: False Evidence Appearing Real

- Feel energised, amazing, and radiant

- Find the biggest block that is holding you back

- Answers are under the doubt and fear - find that inner voice

LEARN HOW TO SHIFT YOUR MOOD

- Find what makes you feel good

- Be happy so that you can believe to achieve

- Learn how being positive and grateful can transform your life for the better

MINDSET

- The power of positive affirmations

- Create a morning routine that works for you to wake up and shine! YOU are not your thoughts.

CREATE YOUR OWN MAGIC

- Set Your Intentions: Decide what you want and go for it!

- Notice Your Mindset and Shift When Necessary

- Use Affirmations that Feel Right for You

- Create a Vision Board of the Life You Intend to Live

Chapter 11
MOVE ON

When it came to having children, I never, ever wanted a girl because I was so scared that I would treat 'her' like I was treated. My eldest boy was born on Mother's Day and I was so relieved that he was not a girl. In hindsight, seeing how well both of my boys turned out, I don't believe I would have treated a girl any different. I'm surrounded by lots of amazing men in my life and it's great. It's obviously helping me.

When I first met Linda Vettrus-Nichols, my Book in 30 Days coach, I wasn't willing to uncover and unwrap the stuff that I'd been through. I was reluctant to do that because I felt that change was a bad thing. I wasn't sure I was ready for that.

Now, I'm letting people know that change is fantastic. It helps you grow and expand. You learn how to take things as they come and decide what is important.

I had all this fear going off in my head, as if, "Oh my gosh, somebody's going to take everything away from me.

I'm happy. I'm not really supposed to be happy.

What if something comes along?

What if we have an accident?

What if..."

It was chaos. It was really chaotic in my head. I couldn't stop myself. I had to say things. I had to let my truth out.

Trust what's around you. The biggest thing is trusting, especially when you couldn't even trust your parents, you know? You've got to find that trust somewhere. Even if you don't believe it, just take a step forward. It could be a step to telling somebody what's really going on. Just do it.

This is the only way you're going to become the best version of yourself. By just being honest with yourself. You'll know when it's right to go and speak to somebody or go on and say something. It doesn't serve you to keep holding back. It really doesn't.

You're here to love and enjoy life. If you're going to hold on to your past, you'll never reach for your future. You get to release it. Don't be afraid...be willing and allow yourself to set yourself free.

Life is easy when you keep it simple. It's that walk or that cup of tea that you love that makes life worth living. It was when I was cooking my favorite meal that I made my final decision to leave home. Stay in touch on the inside. Don't go out looking for stuff, looking for things to fill your empty places. You'll never find what you are looking for if your focus is on external stuff.

If you are a trauma victim, your thinking will automatically be in victim mode. You'll think everything is hard because life has been hard. Life was hard for me for 17 years. And then I made it harder for myself by not letting it go in my head.

Check in with yourself. Ask yourself: "How do I feel?" Not, "How does the person next to me make me feel."

Why did it make you feel like that? Have you done anything wrong?: No, you haven't.

I'm sensitive: And it's okay for me to be sensitive.

Things and people piss me off: It's okay for me to be pissed off. I'm human.

Accepting yourself and doing the simple things which makes life easy for you, is the ticket.

Tapping into what makes you happy is what life is all about.

In all reality, we track back to the past and the future like a yo-yo. As soon as we notice anything that doesn't serve us, we can bring ourselves back to the present moment.

Chapter 12

KEEP YOURSELF FULLY PRESENT

When you're speaking to someone, use their name.

When you walk into a room, take notice of what's around you: What color are the walls? What is that on the wall? What does that say?

Bring yourself back into the now by using all of your senses: I can smell food cooking. I feel really warm. I feel cold.

Something nice is happening: I can sense it.

If something bad is happening, notice it. Observe it. Don't get pulled into it. And then when you feel that you can, just think to yourself, 'What was all that about?'

Start watching and taking notice. Become aware. Because these are the things that are going to do it for you.

If you think about it, we are really good at indulging. Indulging in thoughts, indulging in food, indulging in everything. I had a coaching call with Linda right after seeing my therapist. When I got off the phone, I started binge eating for what seemed like no reason at all. When I took the time to think about it, I was just avoiding processing my sessions.

We can all be more mindful. For me that means at gatherings and celebrations, I only need one glass of wine. Do I really need ten? I've never had ten. I was just being sarcastic.

Ask yourself, am I present when I'm drinking? or "Am I just sipping it away? Just take notice.

Notice your thoughts. It's up to you to start watching them float by like clouds. Don't give them any energy.

It's vital that you do love yourself. It's all about loving yourself. Find things that you love about yourself. Your words will mean so much more than somebody else's. When somebody says, "Oh, you look amazing!" say, "I do look amazing, thank you." Also write those words down when you go home and put them in a jar. When you are having a shit day, you can pull those slips of paper out and read them aloud.

All those nice compliments. These are the words that are going to touch your heart and make you realize that you are a rock star. You're amazing!

Treat every day as a fresh start. Create what you want, including the words and pictures that you want in your head. There's no need to go backwards. You're not going that way. It's time to move forward. Time to think of creating a bright and better future for you, because that's what you're entitled to.

We are born to create. To make things and do things. Not sit in sorrow and sadness and yeah, we all have those episodes; however, we can learn from them and then teach it to somebody else? What can we give that's going to benefit someone else?

Never give up! Never lose hope and in the words of

George Michael,

no matter how hard life seems,

'we should all be praying for time'.

Free Gift:

A 30 Minute Colour Reading

with Suzie!

Inspiration for the day and information

to move you forward, while

transforming your emotions.

Send your request to…

believeachieve320@gmail.com

Let Suzie know the colour

you are choosing.

About the Author

Suzie is a certified happiness life coach for trauma survivors and victims of domestic violence. She has a huge passion to help create a bright and better future for her clients. She empowers them to explore the happiness within, which they have suppressed due to life experiences and conditioning.

Suzie herself experienced homelessness at the age of 17 to escape emotional, mental, and physical abuse. Then for 6 months, lived in a shelter for women and children who had escaped domestic violence, before turning her life around and embarking on a career in mental health and charity work.

She has supported disadvantaged teens by teaching them life skills and self-love. Suzie volunteered for the Samaritans, giving emotional support to the callers who were feeling blue, depressed, or suicidal. She also worked with victims and survivors of domestic abuse ages 5 to 25 teaching them that their self-worth mattered.

Suzie believes that the next generation needs us more than ever. Her mission and message is 'believe 2 achieve 4ever'. She passionately let's others know that they are so much more than their lack of qualifications and that we all have gifts, life experiences, and stories that we can share in order to empower others.

Suzie lives in Leicestershire, England with 'Paddy', her husband of 25 years and their two sons Shane and Alex. She loves walking, traveling, and spending quality time with her family and friends.

CONNECT WITH SUZIE
Instagram: suziebelieve2achieve4ever
LinkedIn: suziewelstead
Facebook: believe2achieve4ever
Website: http://suziesunshine.co.uk/

JOURNAL NOTES

JOURNAL NOTES

Printed in Great Britain
by Amazon

12522982R00037